Gran had come to stay. She had presents for the children. She had bought each of them a Super Squirter.

"Oh no!" groaned Dad.

"A Super Squirter! That's brilliant!" said Chip. "Thank you, Gran."

The children went outside to play with the Super Squirters.

"Wait for me," called Gran.

Dad and Mum watched them.

"Just look at Gran!" sighed Dad. "It's like having a naughty girl to stay."

Gran had a surprise for Mum and Dad. She had some photograph albums.

"What are these?" asked Dad.

"Old photographs," said Gran. "I thought you might like them."

"Old photographs of what?" asked Dad.

Some of the photographs were of Mum when she was a little girl.

"Look at Mum," said Biff. "She was quite pretty when she was little."

"And look at Gran," said Chip. "She was quite young once upon a time."

Biff and Chip went out to play. Gran showed Kipper some more photographs.

"Here I am when I was a little girl," said Gran.

"Why is everything grey coloured?" asked Kipper. "Was it all like that in those days?"

"No," laughed Gran, "only the photographs."

Kipper put the television on. There was an old film about two men moving a piano.

"That's funny," he thought. "They are grey coloured, too. They're just like Gran's old photographs."

The men made Kipper laugh.

At last, Kipper turned off the television. He went to find Biff, but she wasn't in her room.

Then Kipper saw that the magic key was glowing.

"Oh no!" he thought. "I'm all by myself!"

The magic took Kipper into a strange grey world.

"Everything is grey," thought Kipper. "This is just like the film I saw on television."

Two men were trying to move a piano. They didn't see Kipper.

"There is no colour," said Kipper. "I don't like all this grey. I want to go back home. This is a silly adventure."

He banged the key on the wall.

"Take me back," he said crossly. "Or put some colour in this adventure."

The men were still pushing the piano. They had to get it through a door.

"Come and help us," they called.

Kipper didn't want to, but he went across to help.

"We have to take the piano outside," said the big man.

“Then we have to lift it down some steps,” said the little man.

“Now! We’ll take the back,” said the big man.

“And you take the front,” said the little man.

“All right,” said Kipper.

He squeezed past the piano and got ready to help.

“When I call ‘pull’, you pull,” said the big man.

“Pull!” he shouted.

Kipper tried to pull the piano. Suddenly it shot forward and slid down the steps.

Kipper grabbed the top and jumped on.

The piano ran down the street. It went faster and faster. Kipper hung on to the top.

"Now look what you've done," shouted the big man to the little man.

"It's not my fault," said the little man.

"I told you not to push so hard," said the big man.

Suddenly the piano came to a stop. It crashed into a hedge.

Kipper flew over the hedge and landed in a soft garden chair.

"Hey!" shouted the big man. "Look what you've done to our piano."

Kipper was cross. “This is a silly adventure,” he shouted. “I hate it.”

He took the magic key out of his pocket and banged it again.

“I don’t like you,” he yelled. “I want to go home.”

Suddenly the magic key began to glow.

The magic took Kipper home. Kipper was pleased the adventure was over.

But the adventure was not over. Something had gone wrong!

Kipper was a grey colour. He looked like an old photograph of himself.

Kipper did not notice this. He put down the magic key and went to find Biff and Chip.

They were in the garden with Gran. They all gasped when they saw Kipper.

"Oh!" said Biff. "Something's gone wrong. You look grey, like an old photograph."

At that moment Mum and Dad came out of the house.

"This is terrible!" said Chip. "Do something to stop them, Gran. They mustn't see Kipper."

"Leave it to me," said Gran. "You take Kipper inside."

Gran picked up a Super Squirter. She ran towards Mum and Dad.

"Gran!" shouted Mum. "Don't you dare. We're not in the mood for this."

"But I am!" laughed Gran. She began to squirt Mum with water.

Gran chased Mum and Dad round the garden.

Biff and Chip grabbed Kipper by the arms and took him inside.

"Good old Gran," said Biff. "Now let's get Kipper upstairs."

"Ouch! Stop it! What's wrong?" cried Kipper.

Kipper looked at himself in the mirror.

"It's the key," he said. "I didn't want to go on an adventure. Now the magic has gone wrong."

"What are we going to do?" asked Biff.

Kipper began to cry. "I don't want to look like an old photograph," he moaned.

Gran came upstairs.

"Mum and Dad are not too pleased with me. But I've made them a cup of tea," she said.

"You were great," said Chip.

"But what can we do?" asked Biff. "We can't let Mum and Dad find out about the magic key."

Chip had an idea. “Kipper’s clothes look grey,” he said. “Get him to change his clothes.”

Kipper went to his room. He put on a red top.

“Oh no,” said Chip. “Your top’s turning grey. You still look like an old photograph.”

Just then they heard Dad coming upstairs.

"Do something," hissed Biff. "We mustn't let Dad see Kipper."

Gran grabbed some sheets from the beds.

"Pretend you're playing spooks," she said.

"It's dinner time in ten minutes," said Dad.

Dad went back downstairs. He looked cross.

"Oh dear!" said Mum. "What's the matter?"

"It's Gran," said Dad.

"Now what's she up to?" asked Mum.

"Playing spooks," said Dad. "Whatever will she get up to next?"

It was time for dinner. Gran and the children came downstairs.

"Have you washed your hands?" asked Dad.

"And where's Kipper?" asked Mum.

"Well," said Biff. "We've made a little surprise for you."

Kipper came into the room. Mum and Dad looked at him.

"Oh Kipper!" gasped Mum.

"Oh goodness me!" said Dad. "Is this your idea of a joke?"

"You look so … different," said Mum.

“What do you think?” said Biff. “Gran has made him look like a man in an old film.”

“We love it when Gran comes to stay,” said Chip. “Isn’t she clever?”

“Er ... yes,” said Dad.

Mum frowned at Kipper. "Your mouth is a funny colour," she said. "Show me your tongue."

"Oh no!" whispered Chip. "His tongue is grey."

Kipper put out his tongue.

"Oh dear!" said Mum. "Look at your grey tongue. You must be ill. I'm calling the doctor."

After dinner, Mum sent Kipper upstairs.

"Put on your proper clothes," she said. "The doctor can see you in half an hour."

"Oh no!" said Biff. "Now Mum and Dad will find out about the magic key. Do something, Gran."

"I don't know what to do," said Gran.

Kipper went upstairs. Biff and Chip went with him. Kipper picked up the magic key.

"I'm sorry," said Kipper. "I didn't mean to be nasty to the key."

The key gave a little tiny glow. At that moment all Kipper's colour came back.

“I’m glad I don’t have to go to the doctor,” said Kipper. “The magic worked just in time.”

“I think it was always going to,” said Biff.

“You mean it wouldn’t have let Mum and Dad find out?” said Chip.

“I don’t think it would,” said Biff. “Do you?”